When You Go to Kindergarten

REVISED AND UPDATED EDITION

■ ▲ ●

Text by **James Howe**

Photographs by **Betsy Imershein**

HarperCollins*Publishers*

We would like to thank Mara Braverman and Toni-Leigh Savage, who easily and good-naturedly allowed their classes to be photographed for this new edition of the book. Our thanks to their assistants, Josephine Roseti and Sarah Leibowitz, and to all their students, who actually forgot they were being photographed. We also appreciate the cooperation of the principals and schools: Marilyn Wishnie and the staff at Hillside Elementary School, Hastings-on-Hudson, New York; and Lois Gelernt and the staff at Manhattan Country School, New York, New York. Thanks also to Susan Harris, Helise Harrington, and Adam Bucholz.

Special thanks to our editors, David Reuther and Andrea Curley, and our art director, Barbara Fitzsimmons, for giving this book a new life and a new look.

We are indebted to many other early-childhood specialists, principals, teachers, and children who helped us in our research and development of the original edition of *When You Go to Kindergarten*. They are: Dr. Leslie Williams, Dr. James Borland, and Andrea VanHoven, Teachers College, Columbia University; Dr. Selma Knobler, Bank Street College; Dr. Doris Fromberg, Hofstra University; Janet F. Brown and Felicia George, National Association for the Education of Young Children; Shirley Gagliano, Franklin Elementary School, Hewlett, New York; Lee Howe and the staff of Allen Creek School, Pittsford, New York; Susan Howe; and Lois Imershein. Also, Dr. Sheila Terens, Frank Small, Martha Michaels, Priscilla Caine, Ronnie Shulman, Barbara Gold, Gail Pugliese, and Florence Cohn, Number Four School, Inwood, New York; Sandra Roche and Cleo Banks, Little Red Schoolhouse, New York, New York; and Dr. Ellin Carpenter and Vic Klein, Bryant School, Teaneck, New Jersey.

Library of Congress Cataloging-in-Publication Data
Howe, James.
  When you go to kindergarten / James Howe; photographs by Betsy Imershein. —Rev. and updated ed.
     p.   cm.
  Summary: Text and photographs explain what it is like to go to kindergarten.
  ISBN 0-688-14387-3 (pbk.)
  1. Kindergarten—Juvenile literature. [1. Kindergarten. 2. Schools.] I. Imershein, Betsy, ill. II. Title.
LB1169.H58 1994   93-48152
372.21'8—dc20   CIP
                                                                                               AC

First paperback edition, 1995

Visit us on the World Wide Web!
www.harperchildrens.com

With love to Lois and Charles Imershein

Introduction for Parents

Going to kindergarten is a unique experience in the life of any child, even a child who has been to day care or nursery school. In the eyes of most children, kindergarten is "the big school," and entering the big school represents a giant step in growing up. This book is designed to help your child take that step with enthusiasm and a sense of pride.

When You Go to Kindergarten presents a variety of schools, children, and teachers, rather than looking at one school or at one child's experience. As you and your child read the book together, your child will undoubtedly have specific questions about what his or her school experience will be like. You may want to discuss the differences between what is written or shown here and what you know your child's situation will be.

Sharing this book can be especially valuable before your child starts kindergarten, when he or she is curious about the new situation and may be feeling some anxiety. But there may be times throughout the school year when you'll want to go through the book again, addressing new questions your child may have and reliving new experiences together.

Your child will take the step into "the big school" more easily if he or she is prepared and is given support and understanding. Still, letting go of a small hand can be as hard on you as it is on your child. Just remember that when you let go of that hand, you are allowing your child to take hold of something even greater—a sense of himself or herself in the world.

Starting kindergarten is an exciting part of growing up. You will be going to a new place, making new friends, having fun, and learning—all at the same time! If you've been to nursery school or day care, you know what it's like to spend time away from home. But kindergarten isn't the same as nursery school or day care. This book will tell you about kindergarten—and what it's like to go there.

How will you get to school? If you live nearby, you might walk. A grown-up you know well, such as your mother or father, an older brother or sister, or a baby-sitter, will walk with you. And crossing or safety patrol guards will be at the street corners to help you safely cross the road.

If you live farther away from the school, you might go in a car. But you will probably ride in a big yellow bus with other children going to the same school. The bus will pick you up every school day at a bus stop near your home. The bus driver will take you to school and bring you home when school is over.

Your going to school is something for you and your parents to feel good about, even though it may be hard to say good-bye at first.

Your school may be a very big place with long halls. Some schools have stairs. Some have many classrooms and special rooms, such as a library, a gym, and an auditorium or all-purpose room. Most schools have a principal's office and a nurse's office.

Your school may also seem big at first because it is a strange, new place and there may be many boys and girls older and bigger than you. It won't be strange for long, however. Soon you will know your way around, and then the school will no longer seem so big. If you should get lost, there are many adults—teachers and custodians, for instance—who can help you find your way back to your classroom.

Your teacher will be in your classroom to meet you when you come to kindergarten the first day and every day.

Most of your time will be spent in your classroom.
Here there are tables and chairs just your size, as well
as pictures on the walls, books to look at, and all sorts
of things for you to work and play with every day.

On the first day you'll meet the other children who will be in your kindergarten class with you. They're all starting out—just like you.

Name tags will help everyone learn one another's names.

In some schools the bathrooms are in the hall outside the classroom. Your teacher will show you where they are and how to tell which is the girls' bathroom and which is the boys'. There are also water fountains in the hall.

In some schools the bathroom is right in the classroom, and there will be a door you can close. Whether the bathroom is inside your classroom or outside, you will be able to use it whenever you need to.

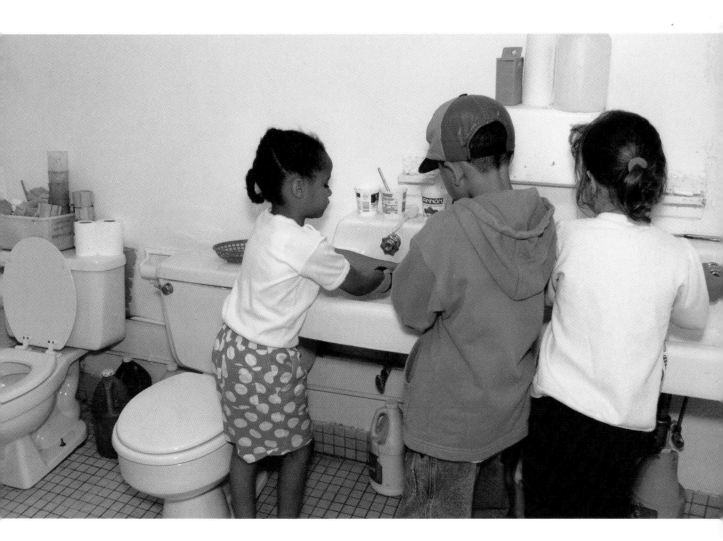

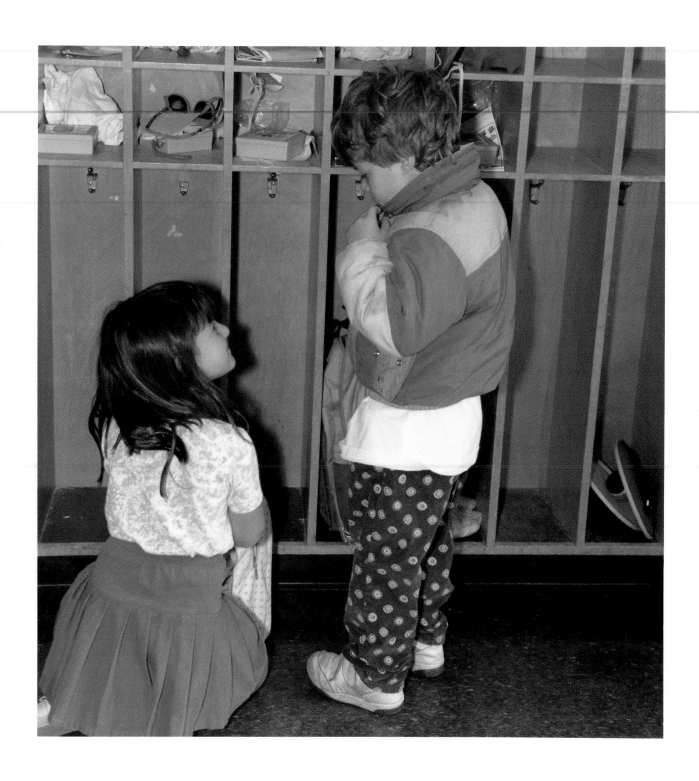

Each day when you get to your room you will
hang up your outdoor clothes, put your belongings
in a special place . . .

and spend some time by yourself or with others
looking at books or playing.

Soon your teacher will ask everyone to sit down together to talk about what the class will be doing that day.

Your teacher will also help everyone learn the rules of being together as a group. It is important to . . .

share . . .

listen and not talk while others are talking . . .

raise your hand to ask a question or give an answer . . .

get in line . . . and take turns.

From the first day of kindergarten in the fall to the last day in the spring, you will have lots to do that is fun and interesting.

You'll learn new things about numbers and counting.

You'll learn about letters and words. Your teacher will help you put them together to begin to write.

Another way you will learn to write is by drawing pictures and then telling stories to go with them. Your teacher will write down the words of the stories for you.

You will get ready to read by listening to stories. Sometimes your teacher will read to you and the other children in your class.

Sometimes you will listen to stories on tape.

And there will be books with pictures that you can look at or read by yourself.

Some children do not know how to read when they are in kindergarten. Other children do know how. This doesn't mean that they are better or smarter. It just means that they are ready to read sooner. Everybody reads whenever she or he is ready.

You'll build with blocks . . .

sing songs and dance . . .

paint pictures . . .

and make things.

You'll learn about
plants and animals . . .

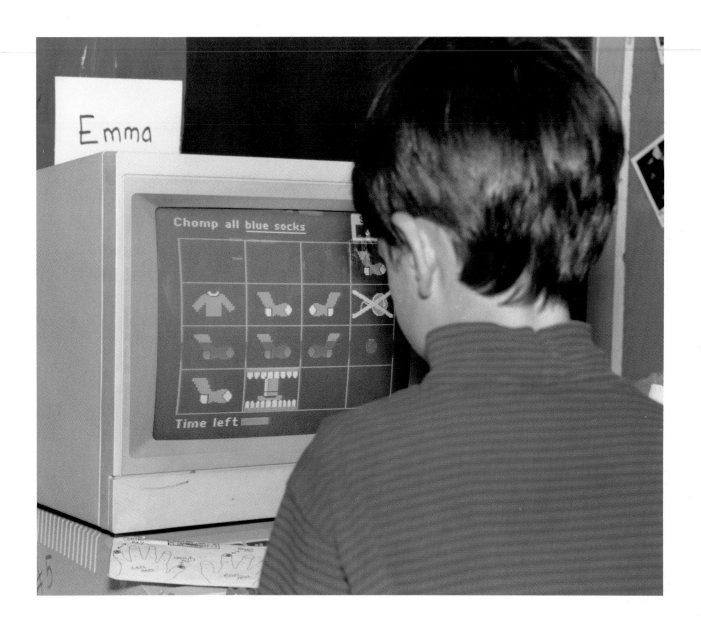

and you may begin to learn
how to use a computer.

Sometimes you'll go outside to learn . . .

and sometimes to play.

It's fun to learn new things. And your teacher will always be there to help you.

There will be times when you can help the teacher, too. She or he will let you know how you can help. One way is to clean up after working or playing.

You will have something to eat—a snack or lunch—
every day at school.

One important thing that happens in school a few times every year is a fire drill. A fire drill is a way of practicing what to do in case there is a fire in your school building. You will hear a loud bell ringing. Then you will line up and follow your teacher outside. Soon another bell will ring and it will be time to go back inside.

Some days will be special. You may go to another room for gym class. Or you may visit the music room or library. You may even go on a trip outside the school.

Holidays and birthdays are always special days. Celebrating them in school will make them even more special.

All of the things you do in kindergarten
will be shared with the other children in your
class. So will all of the special times throughout
the year.

When you first come to school, you may not know anyone, and you may feel worried about this. But soon you will be playing and talking and laughing with the girls and boys in your class.

And many of them will become your friends.

The other children aren't the only ones who will be your friends. Your teacher will be your best grown-up friend in school.

At the end of each day your teacher will help you get to your bus or see that you are picked up by whoever is walking home with you. Some days your teacher will give you papers to take home. Some days you will take home the things you've made to show your family. They'll be very happy to see the work you're doing in school. And you'll feel proud of all the things you can do . . .

and of how much you've grown.

And every day your classroom will be there after you've left, waiting for another day of kindergarten to begin.